SCHOLASTIC

BUILDING FOUNDATIONS IN MATH
SHAPES

Hands-on Activities • Games • Interactive Reproducibles

BY JOAN NOVELLI

NEW YORK • TORONTO • LONDON • AUCKLAND • SYDNEY
MEXICO CITY • NEW DELHI • HONG KONG • BUENOS AIRES

Teaching *Resources*

Cover design by Brian LaRossa
Cover art by Susie Lee Jin
Interior design by Kathy Massaro
Interior illustrations by Maxie Chambliss

ISBN-13: 978-0-439-45872-6
ISBN-10: 0-439-45872-2

Copyright © 2008 by Joan Novelli
Published by Scholastic Inc.
All rights reserved.
Printed in the U.S.A.

1 2 3 4 5 6 7 8 9 10   40   15 14 13 12 11 10 09 08

Contents

About This Book

"*L*ook at me—I'm a circle!" Shapes intrigue children from early on. As they learn the names for different shapes, children use this math language to describe the world around them. Rectangles can be found in the ladder rungs of a slide, triangles on a trapeze bar, squares in sandwiches, triangles in tortilla chips, and a circle in the opening of a birdfeeder. Everyday experiences are an important part of mathematical learning. Children explore properties of geometric shapes while building block structures and learn about spatial relationships as they assemble puzzles. They discover symmetry when observing a butterfly and create representations of the world around them with the use of shapes (such as mapping the place they live). Children are filled with wonder and satisfaction as they observe, investigate, and discover shapes in their world. And making these connections helps them develop confidence as learners in the process.

This book is designed to expand children's shape knowledge through dozens of hands-on explorations and investigations, literature-based activities, games, mini-books, and more—all of which are aligned with the National Council of Teachers of Mathematics (NCTM) Standard for Geometry for Grades PreK–2. The activities help build content knowledge and strengthen process skills, such as problem solving and communication. In addition, they encourage children to make connections to other math concepts (for example, counting the sides of shapes to develop numeration skills) as well as in everyday routines, play, and across the curriculum.

Research Connections

Research indicates that quality mathematics education, when implemented early, results in "learning benefits into elementary school, including in mathematics." (Clements, Sarama, and DiBiase, 2004) Children bring with them significant mathematical knowledge, developed through everyday experiences such as sorting blocks and setting the table. More formal mathematics education at school provides opportunities to extend this knowledge, giving children a needed "introduction to the language and conventions of mathematics, at the same time maintaining a connection to their informal knowledge and language." (NCTM, 2000)

Research supports geometry as a natural focus for math instruction at the early grades. "Our initial evidence indicates that geometry and patterning are foundational for mathematics learning. They are important in and of themselves. They build on the interests and competencies of young children. Finally, they support the learning of other mathematical topics, such as number (from counting the sides of shapes to seeing numbers in rows and columns)." (Sarama & Clements, 2004) The NCTM

Curriculum Focal Points identify geometry as an area of content emphasis at PreK–K, including in-depth exploration of shapes and spatial relationships. (NCTM, 2006)

As children explore these mathematical ideas, it is essential to provide many opportunities to revisit concepts over time. "If we want children to make sense of mathematics, we must provide a variety of experiences that ask the children to think about what they are doing and to focus on critical elements of the concept. It is through encountering an idea in different settings and in many different ways over time that generalizations begin to form." (Richardson, 2004) The activities in this book offer dozens of experiences that build on a set of related skills and concepts and allow children to deepen understanding over time and make connections to more complex ideas.

Assessing Learning

Children come to school with varying levels of understanding about geometry concepts. Some will be able to identify, describe, and name shapes and spatial relationships while others may be learning these concepts for the first time. Use a form similar to the one shown, below, to do a quick assessment of each child's basic understandings. After plenty of in-class explorations of shapes, repeat the assessment to see how the child's understandings have grown.

For continued assessment, place a sticky note for each child on the inside of a file folder. Write children's names and the date on the sticky notes. Then, as you observe and engage in conversations with children, record comments on their sticky notes. Later, transfer these anecdotal records to individual files. These notes come in handy when writing narratives on progress reports and for sharing during parent conferences.

Child's Name _____ Date _____

Shapes and Spatial Relationships Assessment

Shape	circle	square	triangle	rectangle	diamond	trapezoid
Names Shape						
Describes Shape						
Draws Shape						
Identifies Shape in Environment						

Shapes and Reading Success

What does geometry have to do with reading success? Children who can quickly recognize and name letters have an easier time learning to read. (Adams, 1990; as cited in Blevins, 2006) Noticing the shapes that make up letters is one way children develop alphabet recognition. They discover that some letters are made up of circles. The letters *a*, *b*, and *g*, for example, have small circles while *O* and *Q* have big circles. Children who first understand and can differentiate between basic shapes can apply this knowledge to learn about letters more easily. This connection between shapes and letters carries over to writing, as well. As pre-writers, children's drawings reflect their awareness of letter shapes in lines and circles scattered on a page. Soon, they use these shapes to form strings of letters and write their names.

Bibliography

Blevins, W. 2006. *Phonics from A to Z.* New York, NY: Scholastic.

Clements, D. H., J. Sarama, and A. DiBiase, eds. 2004. *Engaging young children in mathematics: Standards for early childhood mathematics education.* Mahwah, NJ: Lawrence Erlbaum Associates.

National Association for the Education of Young Children (NAEYC) and the National Council for Teachers of Mathematics (NCTM) (2002). "Early childhood mathematics: Promoting good beginnings."

National Council of Teachers of Mathematics. (2006). *Curriculum focal points for prekindergarten through grade 8 mathematics.* Reston, VA: National Council of Teachers of Mathematics.

National Council of Teachers of Mathematics. (2000). *Principles and standards for school mathematics.* Reston, VA: National Council of Teachers of Mathematics.

Richardson, K. 2004. "Making sense." In D. H. Clements, J. Sarama and A. DiBiase (Eds.), *Engaging young children in mathematics: Standards for early childhood mathematics education.* (pp. 321-324). Mahwah, NJ: Lawrence Erlbaum Associates.

Sarama, J. and D. H. Clements. 2004. "Building blocks for early childhood mathematics." *Early Childhood Research Quarterly,* 19: 181-189.

Varol, F. and D. C. Farran. 2006. "Early mathematical growth: How to support young children's mathematical development." *Early Childhood Education Journal,* 33(6): 381-387.

Encouraging Understanding

Use these tips to nurture children's natural enthusiasm for shapes and encourage their mathematical thinking in other areas.

◆ Ask questions that challenge children to clarify and extend their thinking, for example, "If I wanted to build a block tower as tall as yours, how do you think I should start?"

◆ Provide time for children to explore and test their ideas with familiar materials, such as blocks, clay, puzzles, and pattern blocks.

◆ Help children connect the mathematics they're learning to their everyday world. For instance, when learning about rectangles, encourage them to find this shape in the classroom and elsewhere in the school (doors, books, cafeteria trays, and so on).

◆ Encourage math connections by incorporating learning into activities children are interested in, such as dramatic play and block building. For example, set up a grocery store where children can explore shapes on the shelves and in the foods (circular can lids, rectangular cereal boxes, spherical oranges, and so on).

◆ Use a variety of assessment methods to find out what children know and what they're ready to learn. Suggestions include drawings, models, conversations, and observations.

Supporting the Standards

Shapes are a natural focus of a math program for young children. The activities in this book are aligned with the following NCTM geometry standards for PreK–2:

◆ Analyze characteristics and properties of two- and three-dimensional geometric shapes and develop mathematical arguments about geometric relationships

◆ Specify locations and describe spatial relationships using coordinate geometry and other representational systems

◆ Apply transformations and use symmetry to analyze mathematical situations

◆ Use visualization, spatial reasoning, and geometric modeling to solve problems

A study of shapes also supports the NCTM algebra standard, which discusses shapes as they relate to recognizing, describing, and extending patterns. As children explore the geometry of shapes, encourage them to investigate how shapes are used in patterns, such as the arrangement of bricks in a wall and repeated shapes on clothing. Helping children make connections in this way lets them revisit concepts and deepen their understanding. They will naturally make connections to other areas of the standards, too—for example, counting or measuring the sides in different shapes to find out how they relate to each other.

Getting to Know Shapes

Investigating Two- and Three-Dimensional Shapes

Activities in this section engage children in building lively word walls, creating rhyming math mini-books, playing games, singing songs, sharing stories, solving problems, and more. In the process, children will investigate two- and three-dimensional shapes—naming and describing them, discovering ways in which they are alike and different, and exploring what happens when they put shapes together and take them apart.

Skills and Concepts Supported by the Activities in This Section

- recognizing and naming shapes from different perspectives
- building with shapes
- drawing shapes
- comparing and contrasting shapes
- sorting shapes
- describing attributes of shapes, including those with lines of symmetry
- patterning with shapes
- taking apart shapes and putting them back together
- relating ideas in geometry to ideas in number and measurement
- recognizing geometric shapes and structures in the environment

As children build with blocks again and again, they develop understandings of relationships among shapes. Two square blocks fill the same space as a rectangular block. Two triangles placed side to side can make a square. A cylinder has a circle on each end. Children develop a foundation for understanding symmetry as they construct a building, carefully adding to one side what they place on the other.

As you observe children in such activities, engage them in conversations that develop math understandings and related vocabulary. Sample discussion starters follow:

- What is the name for the shape of that block? What do you know about this shape?
- What other blocks have something in common with this one? How are they alike?
- What two blocks could you put together to equal the shape and size of this block?
- If you wanted to build the tallest tower possible, what blocks would you choose? Why?
- Which blocks do you think make a good base for your building? Why?
- How are these blocks like shapes you see in buildings?

Word Wall of Shapes Shape Words

This picture word wall helps teach shape names and reinforce math vocabulary.

1. Write the name of each shape you are teaching on a separate sentence strip and add a corresponding picture. Display the sentence strips on a wall, leaving plenty of room around each one. Reinforce properties of each shape by asking questions, such as: "How many sides does this shape have? How many more sides does this shape have than that shape? Which shapes have sides? Which don't?"

2. Pass out large index cards. On each card, have children draw an item or glue on a magazine picture that represents a shape, write the shape name, and sign their name. They may also attach an actual object, such as a sticky note to represent a square.

3. Display each shape card with the corresponding sentence strip on the word wall. Use the word wall to reinforce vocabulary for and properties of shapes. Help children notice the different sizes and orientations that a shape can have. For example, a rectangle can be seen in a small chewing gum wrapper as well as the side of a large building.

4. Add to the word wall as children discover new examples of the displayed shapes and as you introduce new shapes. To reinforce the association between a shape, its name, and spelling, point out each word as you use it in conversations and lessons.

My Mini-Book of Shape Riddles Attributes

As children's shape vocabulary grows, so will this rhyming lift-the-flap mini-book! Predictable text builds word recognition and fluency skills, too.

1. Before children begin to work on their mini-books, show them how to make the pages by following these steps:

   ◆ Cut apart a copy of the cover and riddle template on page 19. Then cut along the dashed lines around the riddle to create a flap.

   ◆ Glue only the edges of the riddle template to a half-sheet of white paper, leaving the flap free to open and close.

   ◆ Read the riddle and complete it by writing in words that describe a selected shape.

   ◆ Draw the shape and write its name under the flap.

2. Give children copies of page 19 and have them make mini-book pages. Let them make pages for all the shapes they want to include in their mini-books.

3. When finished, help children stack all their pages, place the cover on top, and staple to bind. Then have them write their name on the cover. Children will enjoy sharing these interactive mini-books with their classmates and families.

"Mister Sun" Circles Circles & Spheres

This traditional song invites children to use their arms to represent the shape of the sun high above their heads, as they sing about it shining down.

1. Copy the song onto chart paper. Review the arm positions with children (as indicated in each verse).

2. Sing the song together, pointing to the words and using the arm movements to show the sun shining down, hiding, and then coming back out.

3. After singing, compare the shape children make with their arms (a circle) to the actual shape of the sun (a sphere). You might show them a ball to represent a sphere. Discuss how these shapes are alike and different.

(continues)

Teaching Tip

As children create new pages for their lift-the-flap mini-books, invite them to read them aloud during designated times, such as the morning meeting. The class will enjoy listening to clues and guessing the shapes.

Literature Link

Shapes, Shapes, Shapes
**by Tana Hoban
(William Morrow, 1986).**

In this wordless book, readers discover shapes in a lunchbox and on a tablecloth, in an egg and an orange. After sharing the book, invite children to take photos or draw pictures of objects around the classroom or school that represent different shapes. Assemble the pictures into a class concept book for children to explore on their own, with partners, or at home with their families. (On an extra page in the front or back of the book, draw and label the shapes children can look for within the various pictures.)

Literature Link

▲▲▲▲▲

Sun Song
by Jean Marzollo
(HarperCollins, 1995).

Watch the sun come up with a warm and cheery story that is just the right way to begin any day. Let children revisit pictures of the sun and look for similarly-shaped objects in the classroom. Guide a discussion on how spheres and circles are alike and different.

Mister Sun

Oh Mister Sun, Sun,
Mister Golden Sun,
Please shine down on me.

[raise arms above head to form circle]

Oh Mister Sun, Sun,
Mister Golden Sun,
Hiding behind a tree.

[hide arms behind back]

These little children
Are asking you
To please come out
So we can play with you.

[slowly bring arms back up]

Oh Mister Sun, Sun,
Mister Golden Sun,
Please shine down on me!

[raise arms above head to form circle]

—*Author Unknown*

Teams Take Shape Shape Formation

As children team up to make shapes with their bodies, they strengthen creative thinking and problem-solving skills, as well as explore positions in space.

1. Divide the class into teams of three children each.

2. Gather children in an area where they'll have plenty of room to move. Then challenge children on each team to work together to find a way to make shapes with their bodies including their heads, arms, and legs. You might specify the shapes you want teams to make, or draw shapes on slips of paper and place them in a bag for children to select at random. The rules? Each team needs to use all three children for the shape it makes.

3. When each team has devised a way to make its shape, bring the class together. Let the teams demonstrate their shapes for the class to identify. If possible, take photos to share at conferences, open school night, or to use in a class book about shapes.

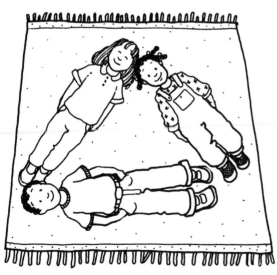

Presto Shape-O! Attributes

After children make shapes with their bodies (see "Teams Take Shape" on page 10), challenge them to do the same with a piece of string. It might not take magic, but using a mysterious cloth and magic wand will add special effects as children demonstrate their skills.

1. Give each pair of children a length of string about 36 inches long.

2. Have the partners work together to shape the string into a triangle. Can they think of a way to make a square? How about other shapes?

3. As the partners form their shape, have a volunteer assistant cover their hands with a large black cloth, wave a "magic" wand over it, and chant something suitably magical.

4. When the pair has formed the shape, have the assistant lightly tap the cloth with the wand and then remove it with a flourish to reveal the shape.

5. After all the pairs have performed their "magic," discuss the different solutions they found for forming each shape.

Sign Up for Shapes! Shape Recognition

Children collect shapes and signatures with this activity.

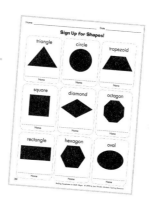

1. Copy a class set of the record sheet on page 20. Cut out the same shapes from tagboard. (You can use enlarged copies of the shapes on the record sheet for templates.) Make sure there is a shape for each child (duplicates are fine).

2. Tape a shape to each child's shirt (like a nametag) or string it on yarn to make a necklace. Give each child a copy of the record sheet. Explain that children need to find a classmate who is wearing each shape on the record sheet and have that child sign on the appropriate line.

3. As children search, encourage them to name each shape they find.

Square, or No Square Categorizing

Are all four-sided shapes squares? Let children discover the answer with this active game.

1. Draw a variety of different-size squares in different positions on index cards, one per card. Make cards for other four-sided shapes that are not squares (such as rectangles, trapezoids, rhombuses, and parallelograms).

Teaching Tip

Use a copy of the grid on page 20 as a template for making signature sheets to reinforce new shapes. Simply mask some of the shapes and replace them with the new shapes you want children to work with.

(continues)

Teaching Tip

▲ ▲ ▲ ▲ ▲

With geometry as a focal point of math instruction in a Pre-K–K classroom, it is important for children to learn to recognize and name shapes in different orientations (for example, a triangle turned so that the vertex is no longer at the top is still a triangle). Look for opportunities to build this awareness and help children make connections between what they know and new situations.

2. Make two signs: "Square" and "Not a Square." Post these signs in an area where children have room to line up in front of them.

3. Mix up the cards and give one to each child (or pair of children). At your signal, have children decide which sign they think describes their shape and stand in front of it. Provide any necessary tools, such as standard and nonstandard rules of measurements, to help children make their decisions.

4. Ask children to explain their reasons for choosing the signs they chose. Use their ideas to write a class definition for "square."

5. Repeat the activity with other shapes, such as a triangle and circle.

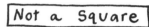

Literature Link

▲ ▲ ▲ ▲ ▲

Cubes, Cones, Cylinders & Spheres
by Tana Hoban
(Greenwillow, 2000).

Everyday objects—such as blocks, balls, bubbles, and ice cream cones—as well as a few out-of-the-ordinary items, are used to teach colorful lessons in solid shapes. Ask children to identify as many shapes as possible in each photograph of this wordless book. Then, with the book in hand, take children on a walk around the school to see how many of the same shapes they can spot.

On a Roll Attributes

What kinds of shapes roll? Which don't? Explore attributes of shapes by examining whether or not they roll.

1. Begin by having children brainstorm things that roll, including balls. If possible, have some balls and other objects (or pictures) that children might name on hand to learn more. Guide them to notice and discuss what the objects have in common. For example, bicycles, cars, skateboards, and trains all have wheels. What characteristics of wheels allow them to roll?

2. To set up a simple investigation, gather a collection of objects, including some that roll and some that do not. Arrange the objects in a learning station. Write the object names and draw simple pictures of them on a copy of the record sheet (page 21). Then copy a class set of the record sheet to add to the learning station. Let pairs of children visit the station to test the objects. Have them record their predictions, results, and comments.

3. After children have had an opportunity to test the objects, bring the class together. Have them use their record sheets and observations to sort the objects into two groups: "Things That Roll" and "Things That Don't Roll." Challenge children to use what they know about shapes to describe similarities among objects that roll.

Shape a Snake Patterns

Set up a learning center with an expandable snake and a variety of shapes to give children a fresh way to explore shapes and attributes.

1. Make multiple copies of the snake patterns on page 22. Color the snake sections, laminate for durability, and cut them out.

2. Provide commercial pattern blocks or laminated die-cut shapes in a variety of colors and sizes, no larger than two inches. (Or use the shapes on page 20 as templates to create shapes for the activity.)

3. Set up the materials in a center. Add body sections between the snake's head and tail to make the snake as long as desired. Then use pattern blocks (or the shape cutouts) to begin a pattern starting at the left end of the snake. The pattern may focus only on shapes, or include more than one attribute (such as color and size).

4. Let children visit the center to complete the snake, using the shapes to fill in the spaces according to the established pattern. If children wish, they can insert extra body sections to extend the snake for additional patterning practice.

Teaching Tip

For young children, it may be helpful to begin with patterns that focus on shapes only. Add in colors and sizes as part of the pattern when children are ready to be challenged with additional attributes.

Headline Cone Hats Shape Formation & Identification

Turn headlines into hats and reinforce recognizing and naming rectangles, triangles, and cones.

1. Give each child a sheet of newspaper. Have children place their newspaper flat on the desk or floor. Ask: "What shape do you see?" Invite them to share ideas for finding out for sure what the shape is. Involve them in counting and measuring the sides. Then help children create newspaper hats by following the steps below. Encourage them to name the different shapes that are formed as they work, as well as to use and respond to positional terms (such as *top, down, left, right, in, up, bottom*).

2. Let children decorate their hats as desired, using colorful paper shapes, curly ribbon, shiny bits of wrapping paper, and so on. Then show them how to open their hats to form cone shapes. Discuss the other shapes children see in their hats. Then invite them to wear their hats in a lively shape parade around the school.

Make a Newspaper Hat

1 Fold the top of the newspaper down to the bottom and crease the fold.

2 Fold the paper from side to side, and crease the fold.

3 Unfold the paper once. Then fold the top left and right corners in to the center. Crease the diagonal folds.

4 Fold one bottom flap up and crease the fold.

5 Turn the paper over and repeat with the remaining flap.

6 Tuck in the flap edges. Secure with tape if desired.

Shoe Box Shape Center Shape Formation

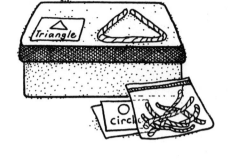

This portable center lets children create and work with shapes again and again.

1. Cover the sides and lid of a large shoe box with colorful felt.

2. Cut yarn into different lengths (from 2 to 8 inches long) and place in a resealable sandwich bag or plastic container. Make shape cards by drawing and labeling target shapes on index cards. Place the yarn and shape cards inside the box.

3. Let children take the shoe box center to their seats to form shapes. Have them choose several index cards and then use different lengths of yarn to form the shapes on the lid and sides of the felt-covered box.

4. When finished (and after you've admired their work), children can peel off the yarn, return all materials to the shoe box, and place the lid on top for easy clean-up!

Transition Time Trace-and-Tell Shape Recognition

Reinforce characteristics of shapes with a quick tactile activity that's just right for filling in time when transitioning from one part of the day to another.

1. Pair up children. Have partners find a place to sit on the floor, with one child facing the other's back.

2. Have children take turns finger-tracing shapes on their partners' backs.

3. Challenge the partners to guess the shapes. Encourage them to visually search shape displays around the room to determine which shapes best fit the ones they felt being drawn on their backs.

Peek-In Pyramids Composing Shapes

These easy-to-make peek-in pyramids let children explore triangles and squares, and how these shapes combine to form new ones.

1. Cut out a supply of 3-inch tagboard squares and tagboard triangles that have at least one 3-inch-long side.

2. Distribute one of each shape to each child in a small group. Invite them to describe the square and tell how they know for sure that it's a square. (Guide them in measuring the four sides to find out if they are equal.) Repeat with the triangle.

(continues)

Teaching Tip

Stock the shoe box shape center with copies of a simple chart picturing the different shapes on the shape cards. Then have children check off the shapes they make. Or, for record-keeping and assessment purposes, use the chart to record dates and anecdotal comments about children's work and knowledge of shapes.

Literature Link

Shape Up!
by David A. Adler
(Holiday House, 2000).

This lively book uses pretzels, cheese slices, and bread to teach lessons on shapes. Children will enjoy following along by making their own shapes. For food alternatives, substitute toothpicks for pretzels, yellow construction-paper squares for cheese, and white or brown construction-paper squares for bread.

3. Ask children to trace the square in the middle of a 12- by 18-inch sheet of construction paper. Then help them identify the side of the triangle that is the same length as the sides of the square. Have children line up that side of the triangle to a side of the square, trace it, and then repeat for each of the other three sides of the square.

4. Guide children in cutting out the new shape, without separating the triangles from the square. (If this happens, they can tape the pieces back together.) Have children decorate the front and back of the shape cutout and then fold the triangles toward each other to form a pyramid. Help them tape three sides in place, and leave the fourth side loose to serve as a flap so they can peek inside their pyramid.

Triangle Put-Together Decomposing & Composing Shapes

How many different ways can children put two identical triangles together? How about three triangles? Four, or more? Let them guess, and then use triangles to find out.

1. Give each child a construction-paper square. Show them how to cut the square in half diagonally. Have children name the two shapes they now have (triangles).

2. Have children trace with their finger and count the sides of each triangle. How many sides are the same? Children can measure to find out, and then use that information to further describe the triangles.

3. Invite children to put their triangles together again, placing two equal sides together any way they like. Let children share their shapes. Have them keep count of the different ways they found to put two triangles together to create other shapes. Then invite them to compare their results.

4. Pair up children and have the partners combine their triangles so they can explore how many ways there are to put four triangles together. Have them keep count and then compare their results with other pairs.

5. Repeat the activity, forming groups of three children (for six triangles), four (for eight triangles), and so on.

Shape Surprise Center Reproducing Shapes

Children use shape pictures as models for creating the shapes with play clay.

1. Make a batch of Perfect Play Clay (see recipe). Then divide the clay and place a handful in each of several resealable plastic sandwich bags.

2. To make shape scrolls, draw and label shapes on small slips of paper (one shape on each slip). Roll up each paper slip, tie with a ribbon, and place in a basket.

3. Stock a center with the basket, the bags of play clay, a safe cutting utensil, and a rolling pin (or cylindrical block).

4. Let children visit the center, select a shape scroll, and then form the shape with the play clay. They can form the outline of that shape with a clay rope, cut the shape out of a clay patty, make a 3-D clay shape, or use their own method.

5. When finished, have children place their papers in a separate container (to be rolled back up and returned to the basket), and return the clay to the bag.

Perfect Play Clay

3 cups water

3 cups flour

3 tablespoons vegetable oil

3 tablespoons cream of tartar

1 1/2 cups salt

food coloring (optional)

Mix all the ingredients in a pan. Stir over medium heat until the mixture has the consistency of dough (about 15 minutes). Allow the clay to cool. Then store in a covered plastic container or resealable bag. (Note: Provide close supervision if making this recipe with children. Let the clay cool before allowing children to handle it.)

Tangram Storytelling

Composing Shapes

A Chinese tangram is a square puzzle made up of seven shapes: five triangles, one square, and one parallelogram. Encourage children to explore the different shapes they can make by putting some or all of the pieces of a tangram together.

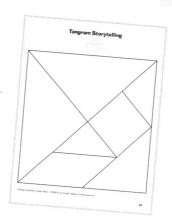

1. Have children color and cut apart copies of the tangram on page 23. Invite them to combine the shapes in different ways to create other shapes and designs.

2. Using *Grandfather Tang's Story* by Ann Tompert as inspiration, have children work in pairs or small groups to tell a short story (one they already know or an original story). Then challenge them to use their tangram shapes to retell the story, arranging the pieces in various ways to illustrate the characters and events.

(continues)

Literature Link

***Grandfather Tang's Story*
by Ann Tompert
(Crown, 1990).**

Grandfather Tang and Little Soo use the shapes of a tangram puzzle to tell a story about two foxes, Chou and Wu Ling, who magically change into various animals. After sharing the story, place the book in a center with a few tangram puzzles and let children use the shapes as they retell the story in their own words.

3. Invite children to perform their tangram stories for the class (or a small group) at a magnetic white board. To make shapes to use on the board, enlarge the tangram pattern (page 23), transfer to poster board, and cut out the pieces. Laminate for durability and then attach magnetic tape to the back of each piece. As children share their stories, they can manipulate the shapes on the white board to illustrate what's happening.

Mirror-Image Math Symmetry

Symmetry is all around—in a butterfly's wings, a fence design, the shape of a leaf, details on a building, and even some letters of the alphabet! Try these activities to explore symmetry with children.

1. Draw and cut out symmetrical shapes—for example a heart and a circle. Then cut each shape in half along its line of symmetry. Hold half of one of the shapes at a right angle to an unbreakable handheld mirror. Let children take turns viewing how the image in the mirror makes the shape look complete.

2. Pair up children and provide each pair with an unbreakable mirror and half of a symmetrical shape. Have partners experiment with the shape and mirror until they can view the whole shape. Encourage pairs to trade shapes to experiment with a variety of symmetrical figures.

3. Have children make their own symmetrical designs by folding a sheet of paper in half and drawing half a design along the fold (such as a paper doll, heart, or butterfly). Let them hold the fold against the mirror to see the complete design. Then have them cut out their designs through both layers of paper, unfold, and look at the symmetry in them.

4. To explore symmetry in the alphabet, write the uppercase letters on index cards, one letter per card. Divide the class into small groups and give each group a set of letters and a small unbreakable mirror. (Make sure each group has at least one letter that has a line of symmetry.) Challenge each group to determine which letters have symmetry in their shape. Bring the class together and let each group present their findings. Ask children if they think the results would be the same for lowercase letters. Let them test their ideas.

5. To extend the activity, go on a symmetry scavenger hunt. In how many places around school can children spot symmetry?

Teaching Tip

▲▲▲▲▲

After children experiment with finding lines of symmetry in letters, let them try it with numbers.

My Mini-Book of Shape Riddles

by _____

Can you guess my shape?
I'll give you a clue:

It _____

and _____

_____ , too!

Name _____   Date _____

Sign Up for Shapes!

triangle

Name

circle

Name

trapezoid

Name

square

Name

diamond

Name

octagon

Name

rectangle

Name

hexagon

Name

oval

Name

Name _____

Date _____

On a Roll Record Sheet

Object	Prediction — Will It Roll?		Result — Did It Roll?		Comments
	☐ Yes	☐ No	☐ Yes	☐ No	
	☐ Yes	☐ No	☐ Yes	☐ No	
	☐ Yes	☐ No	☐ Yes	☐ No	
	☐ Yes	☐ No	☐ Yes	☐ No	
	☐ Yes	☐ No	☐ Yes	☐ No	
	☐ Yes	☐ No	☐ Yes	☐ No	
	☐ Yes	☐ No	☐ Yes	☐ No	

Building Foundations in Math: Shapes © 2008 by Joan Novelli, Scholastic Teaching Resources

Shape a Snake

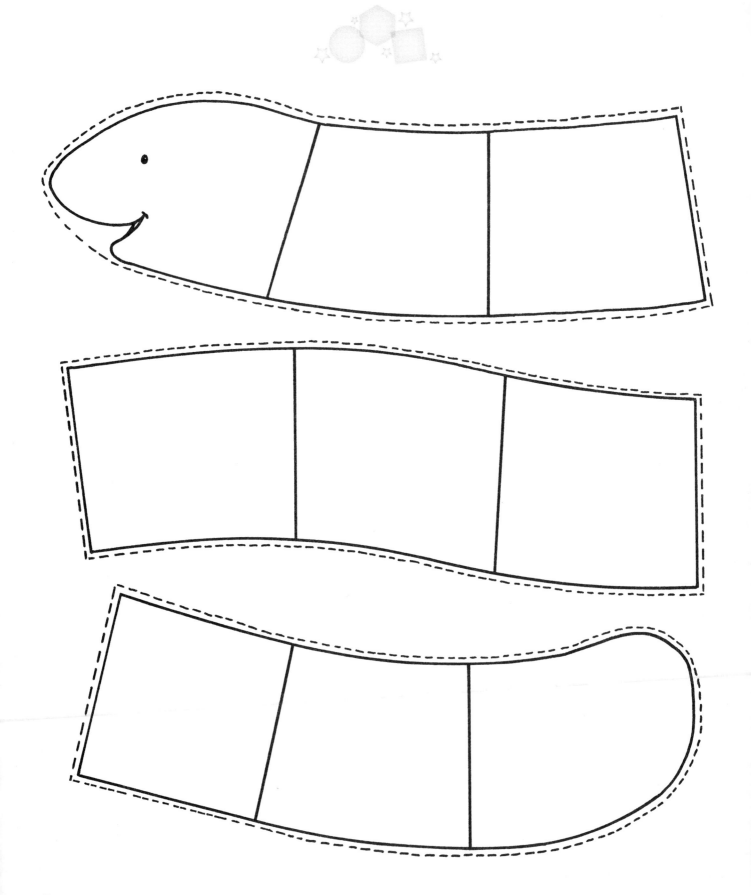

Building Foundations in Math: Shapes © 2008 by Joan Novelli, Scholastic Teaching Resources

Tangram Storytelling

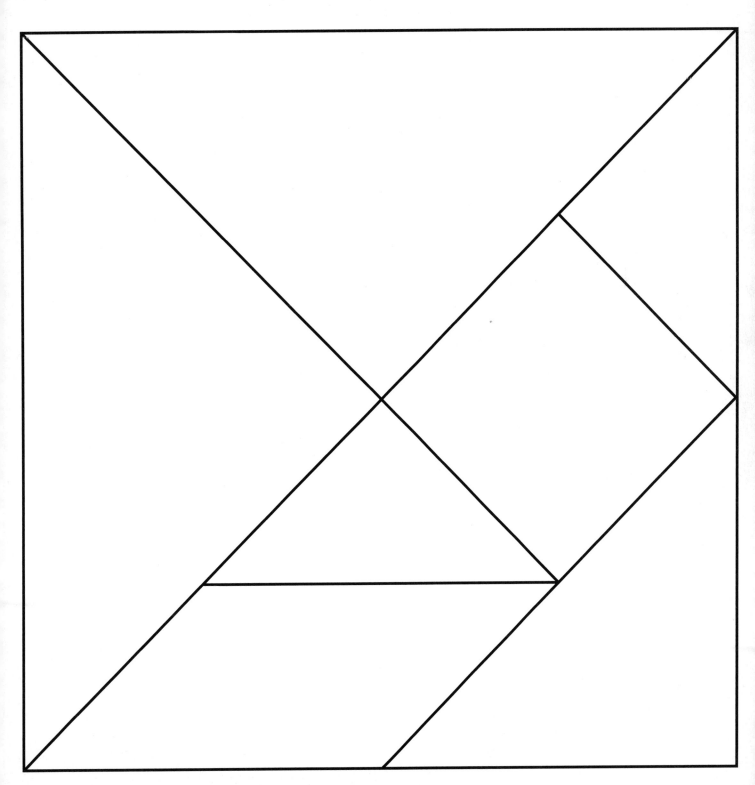

Spatial Sense

Learning About Positions in Space, Directions, Distance, and Location

Above, below, between . . . Learning the language for spatial sense helps children understand the world around them—from the puzzles they put together to the way they follow directions and find things. Coordinate geometry is another way to describe locations. Activities in this section explore spatial relationships, help build language skills for describing and naming locations, and introduce simple coordinate systems.

Skills and Concepts Supported by the Activities in This Section

- developing language to describe positions in space
- describing direction and distance
- finding and naming locations
- using math vocabulary
- working with simple coordinate systems

Dramatic play activities provide great opportunities for math talk. Build language for spatial relationships as children act out stories, interact in a play kitchen area, and engage in other play activities. Sample questions to spark math-rich conversations follow:

- Can you take me on a tour of your castle (or restaurant, house, or other place related to the play activity)?
- Your block tower looks sturdy! What can you tell me about the blocks you used?
- Where can I find the crackers in your kitchen? Are they in the cupboard? Where on the shelf are they?
- How would you set the table for yourself and three classmates? Who would sit where? Where do the cups, plates, and spoons go?

Sight Word Builders Positional Words

The Dolch Basic Sight Words list features many positional words, including *over, down, around, on, right, into, under, out, in, up, before,* and *after*. Reinforce these words and concepts with a picture word wall of spatial sense vocabulary. Illustrations of each term will provide children with meaningful visual connections that strengthen learning.

1. Snap photos of children engaged in activities that represent each word you want to include on the word wall. For example, photograph children sliding *down* the slide, going *up* and *down* on a seesaw, going *across* a horizontal ladder, ducking *under* while performing movements to "London Bridge."

2. Glue each photo to a card. Write the corresponding positional word next to (or beneath) the photo.

3. Display the cards on a word wall. Invite children to use the words in sentences to tell what the pictures show.

Simon Says! Directional & Positional Concepts

This twist on Simon Says lets children move their bodies to learn and practice using the language of spatial sense.

1. Review the rules for Simon Says. Then warm up with a few rounds of the traditional game—for example, to illustrate commands that children should follow, say "Simon says, 'Pat your head'" or "Simon says, 'Hop on one foot.'" Say "Pat your head," or "Hop on one foot" (omitting "Simon says" before the command) to illustrate commands children should not follow.

2. To reinforce spatial sense, play the game using some of the commands shown here (or make up your own). Begin some commands with "Simon says" and leave it out on others. Remind children to follow only the commands that "Simon says" to do.

   ◆ place one hand *on top* of your head
   ◆ place one foot *in front* of the other
   ◆ stand *behind* your chair
   ◆ hop *around* your desk
   ◆ place one hand *under* the other
   ◆ raise your arms *above* your head
   ◆ tap your leg *between* your knee and foot

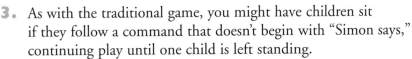
Simon says, "Put your hand on top of your head."

3. As with the traditional game, you might have children sit if they follow a command that doesn't begin with "Simon says," continuing play until one child is left standing.

Teaching Tip

▲▲▲▲▲

Prepare a note with text similar to the following to send home with each booklet:

We are learning about geometry by exploring shapes and the places we see those shapes. Identifying the location of an object helps develop and strengthen your child's spatial sense. Please work with your child to complete this book. You can use the enclosed pen to fill in and illustrate the sentence on each page. When finished, enjoy reading the book with your child. Please return the completed book and the pen to school.

Literature Link

▲▲▲▲▲

**The Foot Book
by Dr. Seuss
(Random House, 1968).**

Left, right, front, back...this book cleverly connects feet to direction, color, number, position, and other math concepts. As you read each page with children, encourage them to notice things in the pictures that are *above, behind, under, over, between, beside, below,* and so on. Try the same thing in the classroom. *What's above the whiteboard? Between the door and the windows?*

Location Mini-Book Exploring Location

Use this reusable, interactive mini-book to make school-home connections and reinforce children's understanding of the language for spatial sense. Families can help their beginning writers complete and illustrate the sentence on each page.

1. Copy page 31 for each book you wish to make. Cut apart the title and text boxes. Glue the title to a sheet of construction paper and each text box to the bottom of a sheet of copy paper. Laminate, sequence the pages behind the cover, and bind together.

2. Show children how to complete the mini-book, beginning with writing your name on the cover. Complete pages 1–5 by filling in the names of objects in the classroom and their locations (for example, "The clock is above the bookshelf") and illustrating the sentences.

3. Place each blank book in a resealable bag, along with a wipe-off pen and a note to families about how to complete the pages with their child (see Teaching Tip).

4. When children return the completed book, let them share it with the class. Afterward, use a paper towel to erase the words and pictures and then send the booklets home with the next group of children.

Mini Picture-Word Puzzles
Positional Concepts

These mini puzzles let children experiment with the way things fit together and provide visual clues to reinforce the language of geometry.

1. Give each child a copy of page 32. Have children color the puzzle pictures, leaving the word boxes uncolored.

2. Help children cut apart the six puzzles and then cut out the puzzle pieces along the dashed lines. Have them put each puzzle in a separate resealable sandwich bag.

3. Let children put each puzzle together. Have them read and use the words on their puzzles to describe the pictures.

Spatial Sense Safari
Positional Concepts

A safari around the school will give children lots of practice in using positional concepts.

1. Copy a class supply of the chart on page 33. Give a copy to each child. If possible, give each child a clipboard to hold the chart. (Or clip the charts to clipboard-size sheets of heavy cardboard.)

2. Review each positional term on the chart. Explain that children will draw pictures and complete sentences to show examples of each word or phrase.

3. Take a walk around the school. Focus on one word or phrase at a time to assist children in learning the language. For example, at the start of the walk, ask children to be on the lookout for things that are "above" other things. Stop periodically for children to draw pictures of what they see.

4. After children have completed their charts, return to the classroom. Then let children write (or dictate) words that describe their pictures to complete each sentence.

Obstacle Course Geometry Following Directions

Set up an obstacle course to teach the language of spatial sense. Leave the course set up for children to use as a movement break or to navigate individually or with partners.

1. Set up obstacle course stations using objects such as large blocks, plastic hoops, boxes, traffic cones (check with the physical education teacher), and a sawhorse (or other object children can safely go under).

2. Make signs to direct children at each station (for example, "Go around the cone 4 times" and "Jump in and out of the hoop"). Add pictures, if possible, to provide visual support for following directions.

3. Let children proceed through the course one at a time, reading and following the directions to go around, in front of, behind, in, out, and between the obstacles from beginning to end.

Teaching Tip

Make pointers for children to use to "read" math around the room. Simply cut out star shapes, label each with a positional word (*under*, *above*, *behind*, and so on), and outline the word with glitter glue. Tape each topper to a dowel and add curly ribbon for a festive touch. Invite children to search the room for things that match the positional term labeled on the pointers (for example, they'll point to a pencil sharpener above the chalkboard tray with the "above" pointer).

Literature Link

Over, Under & Through
by Tana Hoban
(Simon & Schuster, 1973).

Children may be surprised to see how much math is in the everyday activities they enjoy. This book's cover appropriately pictures children scrambling over a climbing structure. Photographs inside capture the math in a young child's world—leapfrogging over a fire hydrant, peeking through a curtained window, and more. Reinforce spatial sense by encouraging children to notice and share examples of *over*, *under*, and *through* during their daily activities.

Literature Link

**Tops and Bottoms
by Janet Stevens
(Harcourt Brace, 1995).**

Children use their spatial sense as soon as they open this Caldecott Honor Book—from the bottom up! In this tale, Bear and Hare try to trick each other out of a shared harvest, with one choosing the tops of the plants and the other the bottoms. After reading, encourage children to use *top*, *bottom*, and *middle* to describe everyday things they encounter (for example, a sandwich has a top, middle, and bottom, and so does a traffic light).

Tops and Bottoms Garden Positional Concepts

If children were characters in *Tops and Bottoms* (see Literature Link, left), what crops would they plant? Have them "plant" a garden to find out.

1. Invite children to suggest crops they would like to plant in a garden. Record suggestions on a T-chart labeled "Tops" and "Bottoms" (based on what part of the plant they would eat). For example, carrots would go under "Bottoms" and lettuce would go under "Tops." Beets might go under "Tops" and "Bottoms" because people eat both parts of the plant.

2. Have children cut construction paper into shapes that represent their crops. Tack a sheet of white mural paper to a wall. Glue brown paper to the bottom half to represent the garden space. Then let children glue their crops on the paper to show whether they are "tops" or "bottoms." Add details to complete the garden scene.

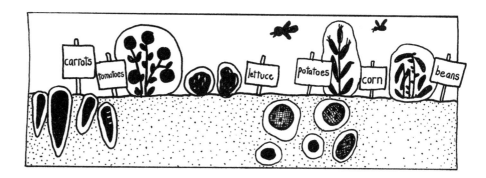

From Here to There Mapping Locations

Build early orienteering and observation skills with an activity that invites children to visualize and map a path from the classroom to another school location.

1. After returning to the classroom from the cafeteria, library, or other school location, ask children to draw a map that shows how to get from the classroom to that place.

2. When finished, invite children to retrace the route with their maps and pencils in hand. (If possible, provide clipboards, or clip children's maps onto clipboard-sized cardboard.) To prompt further observation, ask questions such as "What do you see next to the library?"

Teaching Tip

To simplify the mapping activity, children can map a single location, such as the entrance of the classroom.

and "What is located between the main office and the nurse's office?" As children walk the route, encourage them to check and modify their maps by making corrections, adding details, changing locations of places and things, and so on.

3. Have children use their maps to answer questions that involve spatial relationships, such as: "What is next to the cafeteria? What is above the door to our classroom? What do you pass between the water fountain and Room 201?"

Sundae Assembly Positional & Directional Concepts

Share and discuss *All You Need for a Snowman* by Alice Schertle (see Literature Link, right). Then let children write a collaborative book about what they need to make another fun, cold project—an ice cream sundae!

1. For reference, begin by making a list of positional words on chart paper.

2. Tell children that they will create a story called "All You Need for an Ice Cream Sundae." Have them take turns using words from the list to create parts of the story. Encourage them to be very specific, for example, "You take the ice cream *out* of the freezer. You set it *on* the counter. You lift *up* the cover. You scoop *out* some ice cream. You put it *in* a dish. You pour chocolate or strawberry sauce *over* the ice cream. You squirt whipped cream on *top*. You sprinkle nuts *over* the whipped cream and *around* the ice cream."

3. Write each direction on a separate sheet of drawing paper and distribute to children to illustrate. Place the pages in order and bind to make a book that is a visual treat.

My I Spy Coordinate Geometry & Visual Skills

I Spy books by Jean Marzollo and Walter Wick are full of geometry connections. There are shapes to be seen on every page—from the candy that fills a Sweet Shoppe window (*I Spy Fantasy*) to the streets, signs, and town square in Smuggler's Cove (*I Spy Treasure Hunt*). Invite children to create an "I Spy" scene of their own by using coordinate geometry to place puzzle pieces on a grid.

1. Give children copies of page 34. Have them cut out the grid and puzzle pieces. Then demonstrate how to use the coordinates on each piece to assemble the puzzle on the grid.

(continues)

Literature Link

All You Need for a Snowman by Alice Schertle (Harcourt, 2002).

"Three hand-packed, triple-stacked balls of snow. Hat on top, where a hat should go. That's all you need for a snowman. Except . . ." Rhythmic, rhyming text incorporates language for spatial relationships as readers learn the steps to build a snowman. Once children know what it takes to make a snowman, have them use spatial concepts from the story to create their own story about how to build something else.

Literature Link

I Spy Fantasy by Jean Marzollo (Scholastic, 1994).

Always a favorite, *I Spy* books are full of shape connections. In this book, let children take a close look at the photograph on pages 14–15. Together, identify the shapes that make up the creatures in the picture. How many can the class name? Do children see some shapes in each of the creatures? Do any creatures have a shape that none of the others share? Follow up with the activity in "My I Spy," left.

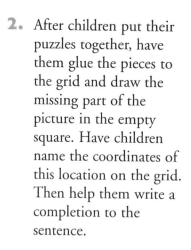

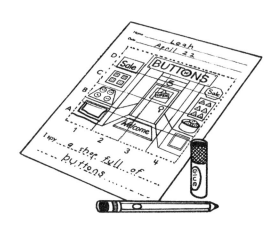

Teaching Tip

▲▲▲▲▲

To let children make their own coordinate puzzles, copy the grid twice for each child. Have children draw a picture on one copy of the grid, label the coordinates for each square, and then cut apart the squares to make puzzles. Children can check their coordinate markings by putting their puzzles together on the other copy of the grid. Invite children to pair up and put each other's puzzles together.

2. After children put their puzzles together, have them glue the pieces to the grid and draw the missing part of the picture in the empty square. Have children name the coordinates of this location on the grid. Then help them write a completion to the sentence.

3. Using the riddles in an *I Spy* book as a model, have children create a rhyme to go with their pictures. Though their pictures will be similar, children's riddles will reflect their own ways of looking at the scene.

Find the Bone Coordinate Geometry

This coordinate game lets children help dogs find a buried bone.

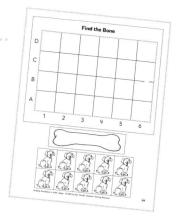

1. Pair up children and give each pair two copies of the blank grid (page 35), one bone, a set of dog cards, a pencil, and some sticky-tack. Have each child take a grid. Assign one child the role of Bone and give him or her the bone. The other child will be Dog and will take the dog cards and pencil.

2. Ask the partners to sit back to back. To play, Bone sticky-tacks the bone over any four consecutive squares on his or her grid, horizontally or vertically. Then Dog tries to locate the hidden bone by calling out coordinates on the grid. Each time Bone verifies that a correct guess has been made, Dog sticky-tacks a dog card in that square on his or her grid. If a guess is incorrect, Dog writes an X in the square.

3. The game continues until Dog locates all four squares that the hidden bone covers. Then partners switch roles and play again.

Teaching Tip

▲▲▲▲▲

For a reusable version of Find the Bone, glue two copies of the grid to the inside of a file folder. Laminate the folder, bone, and dog cards. To set up, provide a wipe-off pen and have players stand a book or other divider between the two halves of the game board. Then invite children to play the game as described.

Building Foundations in Math: Shapes © 2008 by Joan Novelli, Scholastic Teaching Resources

Location Mini-Book

Where Is It?

①

by _____ _____ _____ .

②

The _____ _____

is above the _____ _____ .

③

The _____ _____

is below the _____ _____ .

④

The _____ _____

is between the _____

and the _____ _____ .

⑤

The _____ _____

is next to the _____ _____ .

⑥

The _____ _____

is behind the _____ _____ .

Mini Picture-Word Puzzles

on top of

under

next to

behind

around

over

Building Foundations in Math: Shapes © 2008 by Joan Novelli, Scholastic Teaching Resources

Spatial Sense Safari

Above	Below	Between	In Front Of	Behind
The	The	The	The	The
_____ .	_____	_____	_____	_____
is above the	is below the	is between the	is in front of the	is behind the
_____ .	_____ .	and the	_____ .	_____ .
		_____ .		

Building Foundations in Math: Shapes © 2008 by Joan Novelli, Scholastic Teaching Resources

My I Spy

Name _____

Date _____

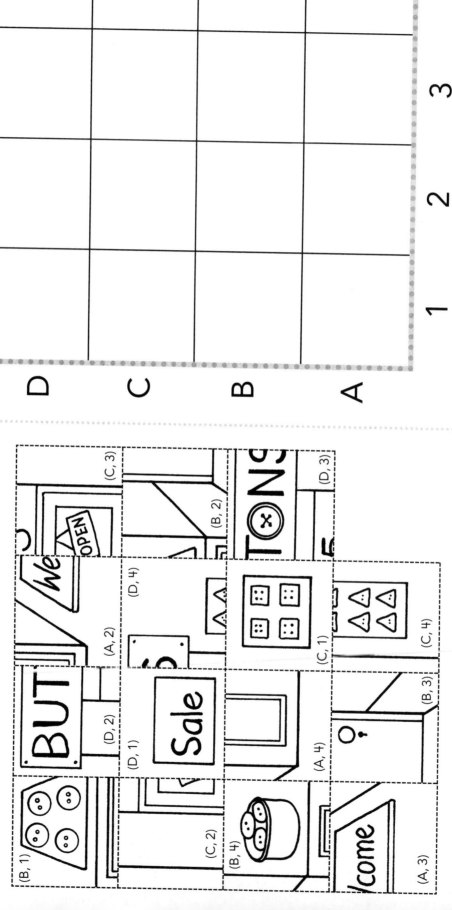

	1	2	3	4
D				
C				
B				
A				

I spy _____ .

Building Foundations in Math: Shapes
© 2008 by Joan Novelli, Scholastic Teaching Resources

Find the Bone

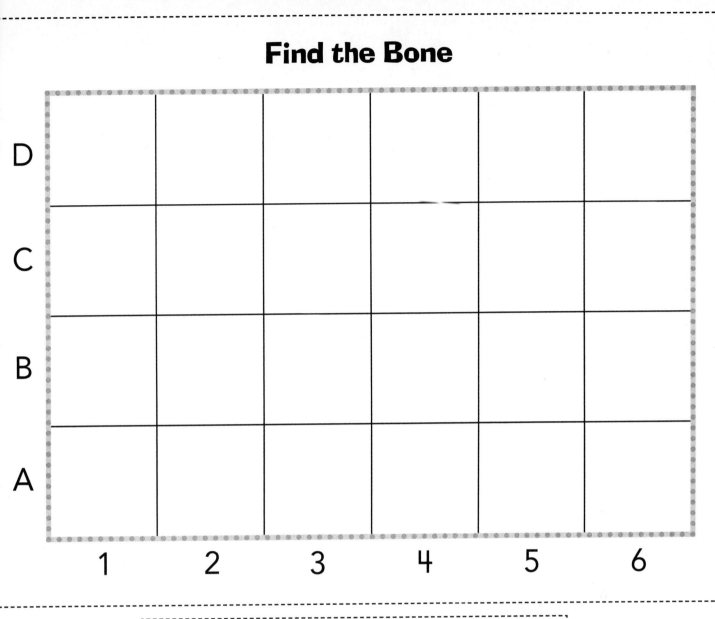

A World of Shapes

Exploring Geometric Shapes in the Environment

Children are naturally aware of and curious about the shapes and spaces around them. A bucket has a round opening that makes it a perfect hat for a head. A box is easily transformed into a train car. Children proudly point out the squares they see in windows and the triangles and cones in pointed rooftops. They spot circles everywhere—in the moon, a plate of pancakes, and the wheels on a bike. In the process of noticing and comparing shapes in their world, children develop an understanding of the ways things fit together, and make connections that will support more complex mathematical concepts. So, while a young child might see the moon and a doughnut as circles, that understanding over time will be modified to differentiate between various similar shapes, such as a sphere and a torus. Plenty of opportunities to explore, investigate, discuss, and revisit shapes will help children refine and extend their mathematical thinking.

Skills and Concepts Supported by the Activities in This Section

◆ using spatial visualization
◆ recognizing and representing shapes from different perspectives
◆ recognizing geometric shapes in the environment
◆ describing locations of geometric shapes in the environment
◆ recognizing and applying flips, turns, and slides

As children make connections between the shapes they are learning about and applications in the everyday world around them, ask questions to extend and refine their thinking. For example:

◆ I see lots of sandwiches at our lunch table today. I wonder if they are all the same shape. What do you think? Why do you think loaves of bread often have this shape?
◆ On our walk today, what shapes do you think you'll see in the buildings we pass? Why do you think buildings often have these shapes? What do you know from building with blocks that helps you understand how buildings are constructed?
◆ How can you recognize a stop sign? Why do you think street signs have different shapes? How does this help people?

Shapes at School, Shapes at Home Booklet

Shape Recognition

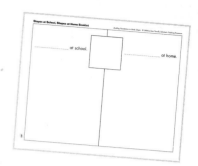

Children can make these two-part booklets to share what they discover about shapes at school and then complete an at-home section to extend their learning.

1. Copy page 43 for each shape you want to feature. Draw that shape in the box at the top and write the plural form of the shape name on the line (such as *squares* or *circles*). Then copy a class supply of each page.

2. Have each child stack and staple a set of booklet pages between two sheets of construction paper. Help them write "Shapes at School, Shapes at Home" on their booklet cover along with their name.

3. Explain to children how to complete the booklet. On the left side of each page, they will draw things they see at school that have the designated shape. They will complete the right section to show examples of the same shape at home. (NOTE: Make alternative arrangements for children who may be unable to complete the booklet at home. You might, for example, work with children to complete the booklets for two areas of the school such as the classroom and the playground.)

4. Let children share their completed booklets. You might pair them up to share with partners, or provide time during morning meeting for a few children to share each day.

The Poetry of Shapes Representation With Shapes

Share Robert Louis Stevenson's poem "Block City." (See Literature Link, page 38.) Then let children build a block city to explore concepts of plane and solid shapes.

1. Let children work in groups to build sections of a block city. To reinforce shape recognition, give each group a sheet on which you've drawn and labeled various block shapes they might use. As children work, have them color in each type of shape they use.

2. Engage children in conversations that reinforce math vocabulary. For example, ask: "What shape do you think you've used the most of? The fewest of? Which of your shapes have sides? Corners? How many have four sides? Six sides? No sides?"

(continues)

Teaching Tip

▲▲▲▲▲

Provide practice recognizing and representing shapes by having children convert their block structures into drawings. Try the reverse, too: Provide a drawing of a block structure and let children construct it. (See Architects at Work, page 41, for more.)

Literature Link

▲▲▲▲▲

Block City
**by Robert Louis Stevenson
(Dutton, 1988).**

This picture book version of Stevenson's classic poem shows the "palaces and castles, temples and docks" a child can create with an imagination and a box of blocks. How many different shapes can children find in the pictures in this book? Guide them to notice cube-shaped buildings, rectangular doors, cylinders in the columns, cones and domes atop towers, and more. List and draw pictures of plane and solid shapes on chart paper. See how many shapes children can spot as they explore the book.

3. Invite children to show where they used the shapes they colored in. Encourage them to name each shape and describe its attributes as they point it out in their construction.

4. If possible, take photographs of the city as it is constructed. Use the photos to make a picture book with children about the shapes they see in their block city.

To Market, To Market Identifying Shapes in Context

To reinforce geometry skills, set up a market in your dramatic play area, complete with shopping baskets and stocked shelves (use clean, empty food containers, such as cereal boxes, yogurt cups, and juice concentrate cans). Then try these activities:

◆ Have children notice how items are arranged on shelves. Which items are stacked? Why are some groceries stacked and others aren't? Invite children to explore and share their ideas. (You might also have them arrange—or rearrange—items to test their ideas.)

◆ Encourage partners to take turns choosing items from the shelves, naming the shapes they see on the items, and then adding them to a shopping basket. Or challenge them to try to find items that have the same shape (such as a chip canister and oatmeal canister).

◆ When unpacking groceries, have one child remove an item and then have his or her partner find something that has a shape in common with that item.

For a school-home connection, send a note to families describing how they can try some of these activities with their child while grocery shopping together. Include in the letter that fun, easy activities such as these help children connect their knowledge of shapes to the world around them.

Math in My Lunch! Shape Identification

What's for lunch? Whether children eat the school lunch or bring theirs from home, they are bound to see all sorts of shapes in it!

1. To create journals, ask children to cut apart multiple copies of the record sheet on page 44. Have them stack and staple the pages between two sheets of construction paper and then decorate the cover.

2. After lunch, demonstrate how to complete a page by thinking aloud about the shapes in your own lunch. For example, you might say "My sandwich had a square shape. I'm going to color in a

box for *square* to show that I ate square bread. I'll color in a box for *circle*, too, to show the shape of my cucumber slices." Then write a sentence about the shapes in your lunch (for example, *I ate a square sandwich and cucumber circles*).

3. After lunch each day, invite children to complete a page in their journal, coloring in boxes to represent the shapes they ate and writing (or dictating) sentences about the shapes. They might spot a dome in a sandwich bun or scoop of potatoes, a triangle in a cracker, rectangles in a fish stick (also a rectangular prism), and so on.

Dominoes Shape Up

Matching Shapes in Context

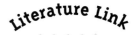

In this twist on dominoes, children match shapes in pictures of everyday objects to make an attribute chain.

1. Copy the domino patterns (page 45) onto tagboard, laminate, and cut apart. Divide the dominoes evenly among two to three players.

2. Before play, explain that children will try to match pictures on their dominoes by the shapes that the pictures share (for example, the ice cream cone and glass share a cylinder shape).

3. Have the first player set a domino in the center of the playing area. The next player checks his or her dominoes to find a picture that shares a shape found in a picture on the starter domino. If a match is found, the player names the shape and places that end of the domino next to the one it matches (lining them up at an edge). If no shape is found, play moves to the next player. Play continues until children have linked all their dominoes or no more matches can be made.

4. If desired, make extra sets of the dominoes for children to take home and play with their families. Store each set in a resealable bag.

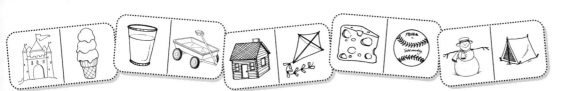

For a variation, make a new set of dominoes by cutting a supply of 4- by 6-inch index cards into three parts each (2- by 4-inches). Glue small pictures (or parts of pictures) from catalogs and magazines to the ends of each domino. The pictures should have shapes embedded in them, for example, a picture of a toaster might show rectangular openings for toast. To play, have children match shape attributes in the pictures.

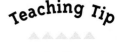

Literature Link

▲▲▲▲▲

Castle
by David McCauley
(Houghton Mifflin, 1977).

In this Caldecott Honor Book, readers can follow the brick-by-brick construction of a magnificent castle. Intricate illustrations reveal different shapes coming together as the castle is created. After enjoying this book, children may be inspired to examine shapes in the architecture around them. They might diagram a favorite building, labeling parts and shapes they see.

Lift-the-Flap Castle   Shapes in Context & Shape Vocabulary

A castle may not be an ordinary sight to see, but with this peek-through castle, you can reinforce children's vocabulary for common shapes.

1. Give each child a copy of pages 46–47. Have children cut out and color the castle and add details to personalize it.

2. Help children cut along the dashed lines to create eight flaps. Have them glue only the back edges of the castle to the page labeled with shapes, making sure the edges line up and each word or phrase is directly under the correct flap.

3. Let children explore their castle, naming the shapes they see on the outside, then lifting the flap to peek inside and read the corresponding shape word.

4. For a whole-class extension, have children work together to draw (on a large sheet of paper) a representation of the school's exterior. Cut flaps around recognizable shapes and glue the drawing to another sheet of paper along the edges only. Lift each flap and label the shape underneath.

Balls and Rings   3-D Circular Shapes

Children often describe balls, wheels, oranges, bagels, and the sun as circles. From a two-dimensional perspective, these objects do look like circles. But in 3-D, their shapes are actually spheres (balls) and toruses (rings). Plan a treasure hunt to help children begin to recognize attributes of familiar, but sometimes confusing, shapes.

1. Divide the class into small groups. Give each group a ball and a ring (such as from a ring-toss game).

2. Have children look around the room, in books, in their cubbies—anywhere you say it's okay—to find examples of each shape. Have children gather the items if small, or draw pictures of them if they're not portable.

3. Bring children together to share their treasures. Then use a chart to sort the objects into three groups: "Shaped Like a Ball," "Shaped Like a Ring," and "Not Shaped Like a Ball or Ring." Guide children to discover the attributes that make a ball different from a ring. Discuss how other objects might be similar to a ball or a ring, but not be the same shape. For example, a paper-towel tube can roll like a ball, but it is not a sphere.

Shapes and Signs

Shape Recognition

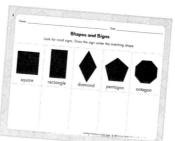

Combine a lesson on road signs and safety with one on shapes.

1. Copy the record sheet on page 48 and clip it onto a clipboard. Share the shapes shown on the record sheet with children, counting the sides and angles in each shape. Then tell children that they will look for road signs that match these shapes. Take a walk that will allow children to safely view as many road signs as possible.

2. When children spot a matching sign shape, stop to discuss what the sign means. Then draw it in on the record sheet in the corresponding column. (Include any words or pictures that appear on the sign.) For example, a "School Crossing" sign matches the pentagon, and a "Stop" sign matches the octagon.

3. After returning to the classroom, review the signs with children. Discuss why using specific shapes for certain signs can be helpful in communicating important messages and making the roads safe.

Architects at Work   3-D Representations

Architects work with engineers, builders, and others to translate geometric designs on paper into actual structures. It's fun and a challenge for children to try doing the same!

1. Set up a block center and display a series of designs—structures that children can build with available blocks. You can create designs on large-grid graph paper to provide consistency of scale.

2. As children work, invite them to tell how they decide which shapes to use. Encourage use of mathematical language. For example, ask: "What shape do you think comes first? How do you know? How is this shape like the drawing you see? What's different?"

(*continues*)

Take copies of the record sheet (page 48) along on field trips to keep track of the sign shapes children see as they travel. Or invite children to take home individual copies to complete with their families. (You might send home a note explaining to families how to fill out the record sheet.)

Literature Link
▲▲▲▲▲

I Read Signs and ***I Read Symbols***
by Tana Hoban
(Greenwillow, 1983).

Colorful photographs introduce children to signs in the world around them. To help children connect the signs to individual shapes, distribute construction-paper shapes represented by signs in the books (one per child). As you read, ask children to hold up their shapes when they see matching sign shapes. You might point out that some signs combine different shapes (for example, a square "No Left Turn" sign has a circle symbol on it).

Teaching Tip

▲ ▲ ▲ ▲ ▲

"In order to contextualize mathematics in real life. . . focus on how carpenters, candy sellers, or fishermen use mathematics. . . ." (Varol & Farran, 2006) To encourage meaningful mathematical connections, invite people who use geometry in their work to talk with the class about what they do. Architects, engineers, electricians, plumbers, designers, carpenters, clothing-makers, gardeners and landscapers, city planners, and chefs are just a few careers to consider.

Literature Link

▲ ▲ ▲ ▲ ▲

**Color Zoo
by Lois Ehlert
(HarperCollins, 1989).**

Colors, shapes, and cutouts come together to create ever-changing animals in this dazzling Caldecott Honor Book. A tiger becomes a mouse; a lion becomes a goat. Can children discover how? (Hint: have them look for the way shapes are turned.) Shapes are labeled, letting readers make connections between the shapes and their printed names.

3. Invite children to estimate how big a structure will be. The blocks represented on the paper may be much smaller than the actual blocks, but children can look at how big blocks are relative to one another to estimate the size of the completed structure. When finished, have children compare their structure to the design on paper.

4. Extend and support children's growing understanding of the way they can use geometric shapes to represent and describe the world around them by providing plenty of blocks, large-square graph paper, and other materials for hands-on explorations. Then invite children to construct and draw their own architectural designs on a grid for classmates to build.

Geometry Zoo Representation With Shapes

Using the concept book *Color Zoo* by Lois Ehlert as inspiration (see Literature Link, left), invite children to transform shapes into animals.

1. Provide tagboard templates for shapes represented in the book. Then let children trace and cut out construction-paper shapes and experiment with arranging them to create animal pictures. (Children might discover that they need to modify some shapes or cut new ones to make their ideas work.)

2. After creating their animals, have children glue the shapes in place. Then challenge them to make an identical set of shapes to use in creating a new animal. Take this opportunity to demonstrate how children can slide, flip, and turn their shapes to get different effects. (You might use pattern blocks to model different positions of the same shape.)

3. Display each child's animal pair together. Guide children to notice that while a shape's position may have changed from one design to the other, its form and size remain the same. To take the learning further, point out examples of slides, flips, and turns in children's work.

Building Foundations in Math: Shapes © 2008 by Joan Novelli, Scholastic Teaching Resources

at home.

at school.

Name _____   Date _____

Math in My Lunch!

Color a square for each shape that you found in your lunch.

triangle	square	circle	rectangle	dome	Other:

Write about the shapes in your lunch.

_____

_____

_____

_____

Dominoes Shape Up

Lift-the-Flap Castle

Lift-the-Flap Castle

triangle

circle

cone

cylinder

rectangle

square

trapezoid

cube

Building Foundations in Math: Shapes © 2008 by Joan Novelli, Scholastic Teaching Resources

Shapes and Signs

Look for road signs. Draw the sign under the matching shape.

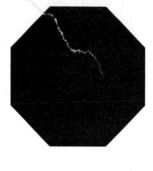				
octagon	pentagon	diamond	rectangle	square

Building Foundations in Math: Shapes   © 2008 by Joan Novelli, Scholastic Teaching Resources